ONE, TWO, THREE :

My Sister, My Brother, and Me

AD Owens

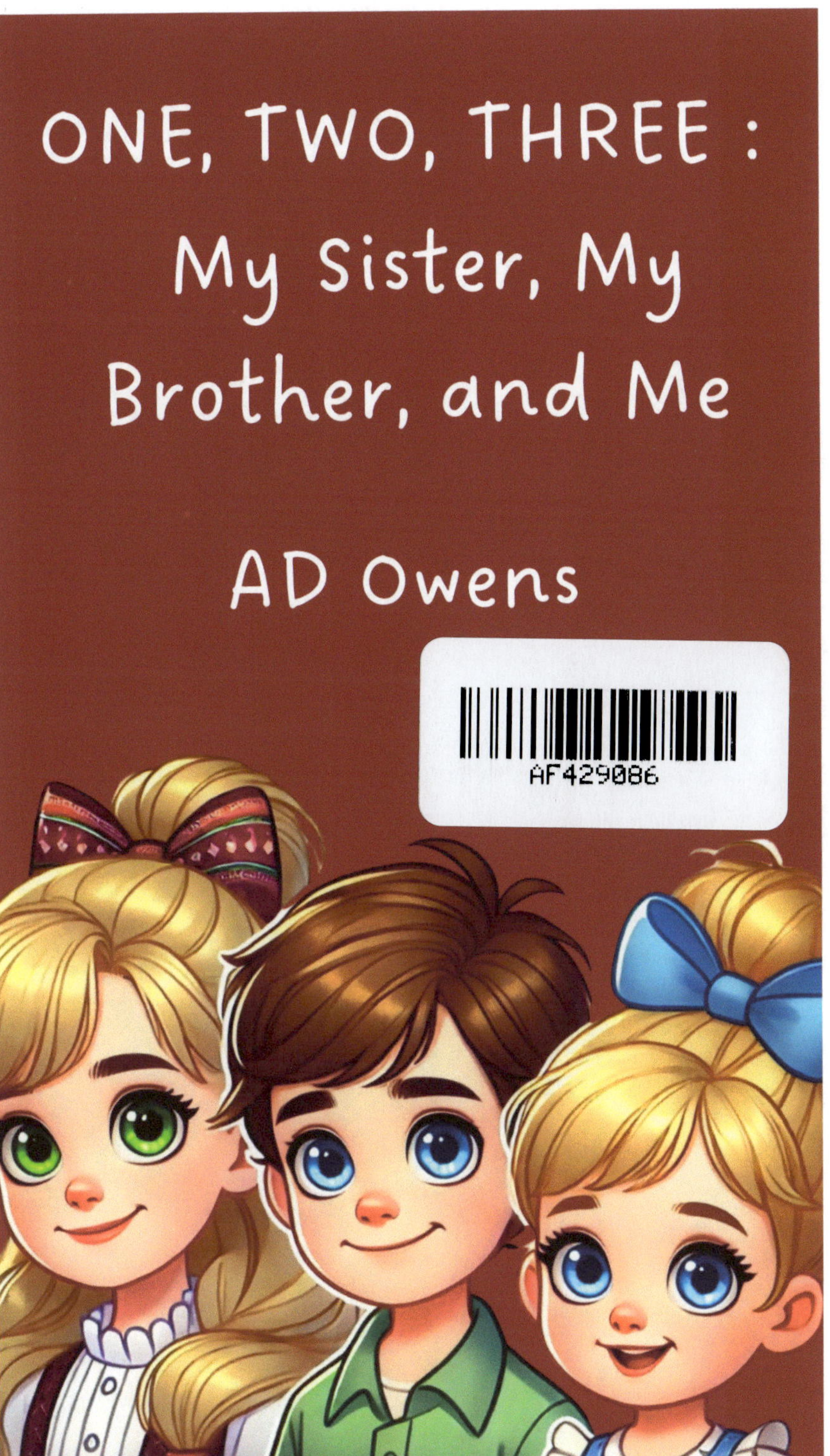

"They say that no matter how old you become, when you are with your siblings, you revert back to childhood." - Karen White

For Beth and John

Because of you, I will always have a friend, and I will never be alone. I am honored to be your sister, and blessed to have you in my corner for life.

Love you always - NayNay

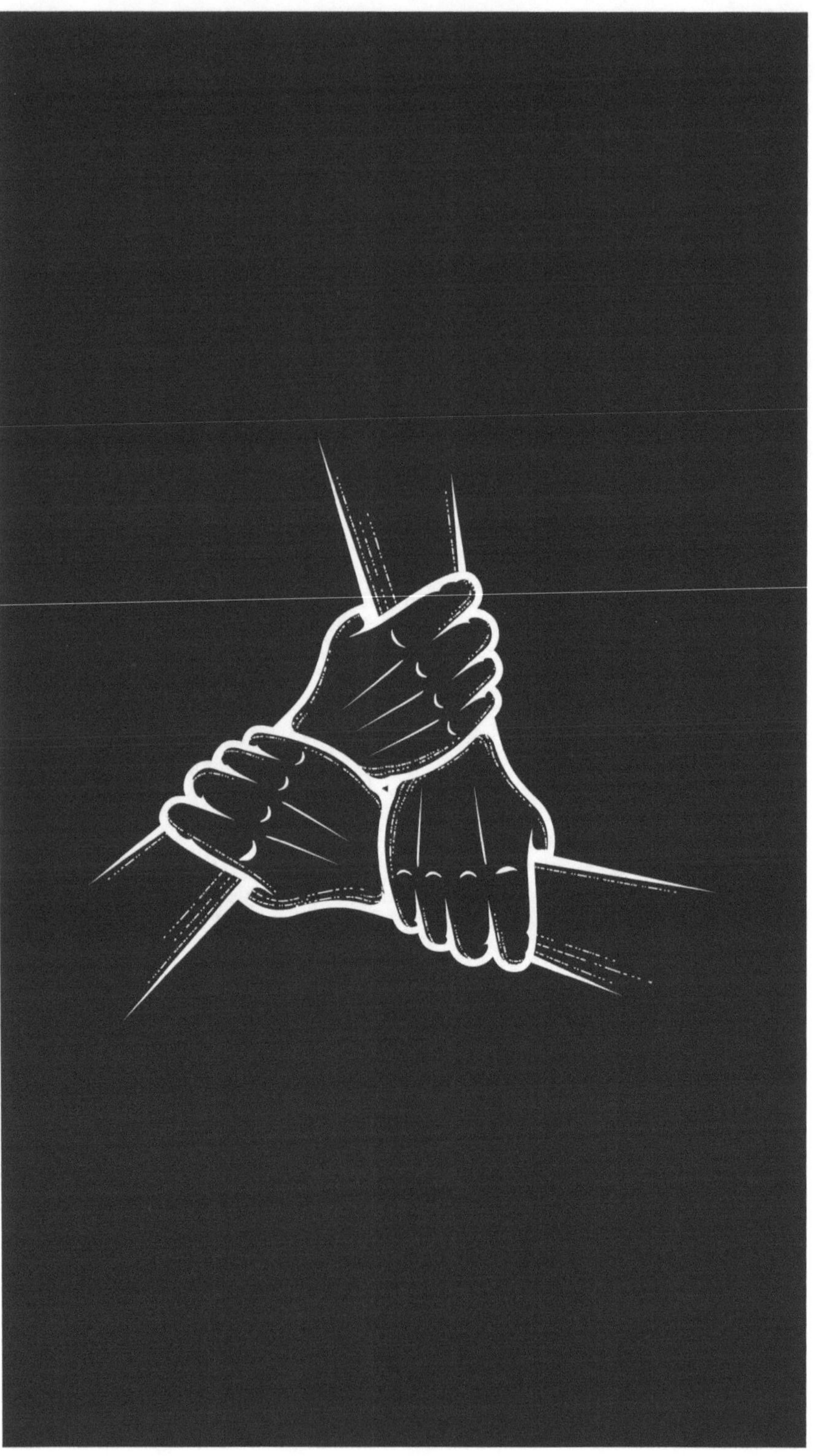

Let me tell you a story of three
siblings so bright,

Beth, John, and Anna—oh, what
a sight!

They giggled, they played, they
sometimes disagreed,

but through it all, they were
family indeed.

With each little prank, each laugh
and tear,

they grew up together, year
after year.

So sit back, relax, and come
along with me,

through the tales of

Beth, John, and Anna :

siblings 1, 2, and 3.

Beth was the oldest,

with John in between.

Then came little Anna,

the baby and family queen.

The following stories are silly

and certainly true,

and through each one, their

bond always grew.

One day dear John had a trick in.
his head.

"Anna, try this!" he mischievously said.

He handed Anna a pearl from Mom's
pretty things,

"Pop it in your nose, just see what
it brings!"

Anna, so eager, gave it a try.

But, oh no! That pearl got stuck so high!

Mom and Dad rushed Anna to
the hospital quick.

Little Anna learned the hard way about
falling for tricks!

Then came a day when Beth had
a plan.

With a giggle, she said, "We're
pranking the man!"

Beth and her friend gave little
Anna the car's horn to toot,

to scare their teacher in a
wild pursuit!

Anna, just four, thought it was
a game,

pressed the horn down, not
thinking of shame.

But the teacher glaring with
eyes open wide,

didn't find it funny and
angrily replied!

One day Beth and John told Anna,
"Hide, and don't make a sound,

playing this game is fun hiding and
searching all around!"

Anna, excited, ran quick to the spot.

The closet she hid, in a bundle
she got.

Hours went by, and she fell
fast asleep.

For this prank, Beth and John
tried not to make a peep.

Mom and Dad were so worried.

They searched for hours on end,

'til Beth and John reluctantly
confessed.

Oh! What trouble they were in!

Now the years have gone by,
and we've all grown tall,

no longer those kids running
and jumping down the hall.

Through all the adventures,
the laughter, pranks,
and fun,

We've grown even closer—our
bond can't be undone.

Beth, the big sister,
beautiful and
incredibly smart,

John, with his smile, so charming and full of heart,

and me, still the baby,
making up one of
three parts.

From pranks to mischief, to
laughter and tears,

We've walked side by side
through all of the years.

Now decades have passed,
and life's gone its way,

but our bond as siblings is
here to stay.

We've faced ups and downs,
and passed every test.

We know that together we've
been truly blessed.

Nothing comes before our
family - that's certainly true,

as three hearts beat as one
in this sibling crew.

Sitting here now, thinking
of memories so bright,

our love is still strong, and
our bond still tight.

Time may continue to pass,
still we will forever be :

One, Two, Three - my sister,
my brother, and me.

Beth
Anna
John

Beth

Anna

John

About the Author

AD Owens grew up surrounded by laughter, love, and the endless adventures that come with being the youngest of three siblings. Inspired by the heartwarming (and often mischievous!) moments shared with her sister Beth and brother John, she decided to capture these childhood memories in this delightful tale.

As a storyteller, AD Owens believes in the magic of family, the joy of sibling bonds, and the importance of cherishing the playful, unforgettable moments that shape us. She enjoys passing on these stories and values to the next generation, encouraging children to embrace the fun and love that comes from growing up with siblings.

In "ONE, TWO, THREE : My Sister, My Brother, and Me," AD (Anna) shares the ups and downs of sibling life, weaving together laughter and heartfelt moments in a story that resonates with readers young and old.

Through her charming and personal writing style, she hopes to remind families everywhere that no matter the pranks or rivalries, the bond between siblings is one of life's greatest treasures.

Siblings One, Two, and Three :
John (left) Anna (middle) Beth (right)
pictured in front of Bryant-Denny
Stadium in Tuscaloosa, Alabama.

ROLL TIDE!

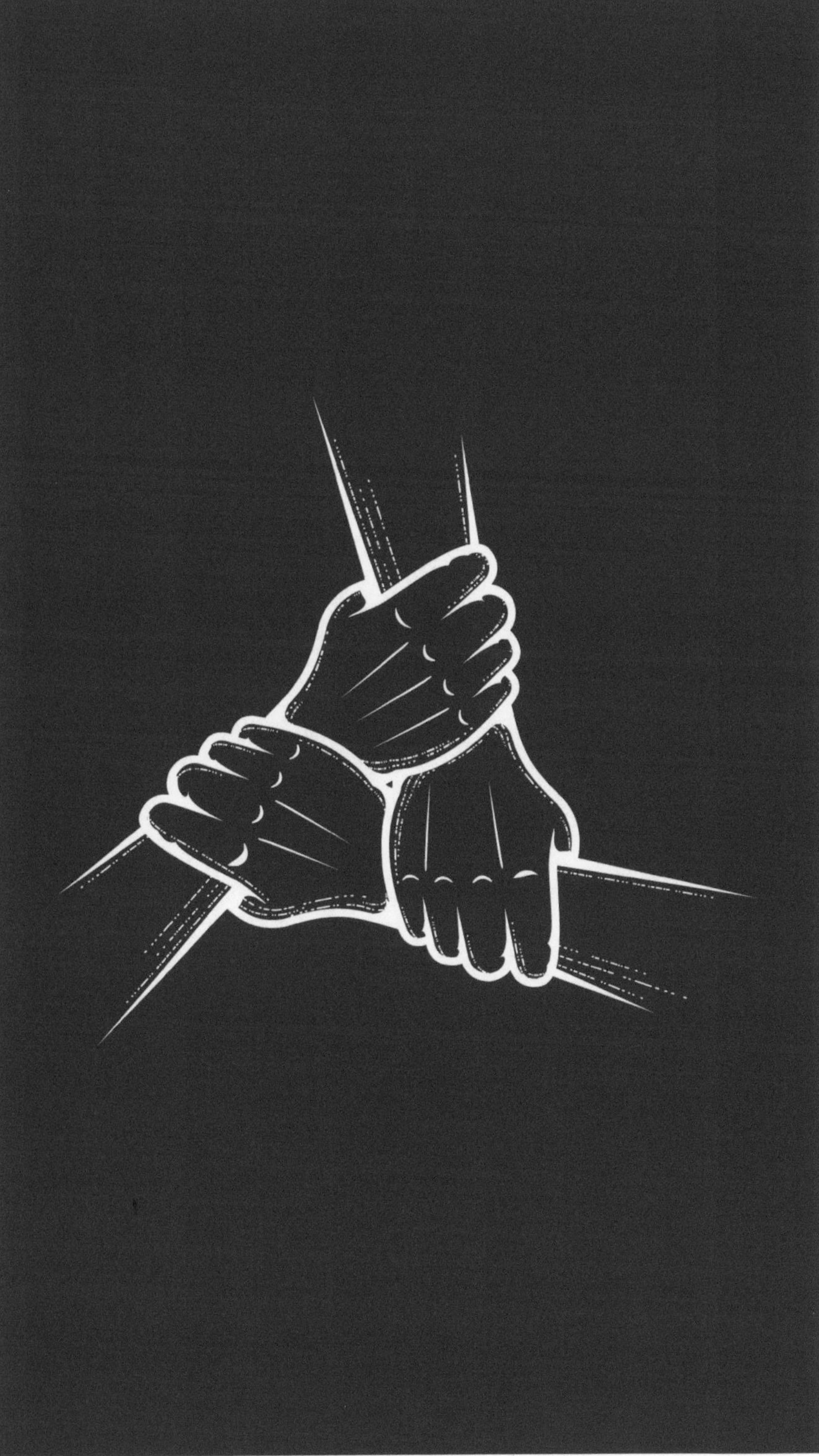